Amazing Mysteries
STRANGE PLACES

Anne Rooney

A⁺

Smart Apple Media

Smart Apple Media
P.O. Box 3263, Mankato, MN 56002

Printed in the United States of America

Library of Congress Cataloging-in-Publication Data

Rooney, Anne.
  Strange places / Anne Rooney.
     p. cm. -- (Amazing mysteries)
  Includes index.
  ISBN 978-1-59920-366-9 (hardcover)
  1. Haunted places--Juvenile literature. 2. Curiosities and wonders--Juvenile literature. I. Title.
  BF1461.R66 2010
  001.94--dc22

                              2008053335

Created by Q2AMedia
Editor: Honor Head
Art Director: Rahul Dhiman
Designer: Harleen Mehta
Picture Researcher: Shreya Sharma
Line Artist: Sibi N. Devasia
Coloring Artist: Mahender Kumar

Picture credits
t=top b=bottom c=center l=left r=right

Cover Image: Maugli/ shutterstock, Inset: Shutterstock

Insides: The Bridgeman Art Library/ Photolibrary: 5, O. Alamany & E. Vicens/ Corbis: 6, Nik Wheeler / Alamy: 8, Jim Sugar/ Corbis:
9c, Fatih Kocyildir/ Shutterstock: 10b, T. Bradford/ iStockphoto: 11, Julia Chernikova/ Shutterstock: 12t, Svetlana Privezentseva/
Shutterstock: 13, Silvrshootr/ iStockphoto: 14, Jarno Gonzalez Zanraonandia/ Shutterstock: 15, Martin Gray/ National Geographic/
Getty Images: 16, JTB Photo/ Photolibrary: 17t, Chris Langridge/ Sygma/ Corbis: 18b, Pascal Deloche/ Godong/ Corbis: 19, Matt
Trommer/ Shutterstock: 20, Craig Fujii/ Associated Press: 21t, Edward J. Bochnak: 22, Edward J. Bochnak: 23tr, Bryan Busovicki/
Shutterstock: 23c, TravelibUK / Alamy: 26, Laura Glickstein/ Shutterstock: 28, James Montgomery/ Photolibrary: 29

Q2AMedia Art Bank: Title Page, 4, 7, 10, 24, 25, 27, 31.

9 8 7 6 5 4 3 2 1

Contents

Mystery and Magic

The world is full of strange places—but some are stranger than others. Odd things that are hard to explain can happen in places that at first seem quite ordinary.

Now You See It . . .

. . . now you don't! Some of the places in this book have mysteriously disappeared. Cities have vanished beneath the sea, or been covered by jungle too thick for explorers to cut through. Perhaps even a whole continent has been swallowed up.

The Right Lines?

Many ancient sites in Europe are said to line up, lying along straight lines that criss-cross the country. These lines are called **ley lines**. Some people think ley lines have special powers and channel energy of some sort. Perhaps people long ago lined up their sacred sites to tap into this mysterious energy.

Scotland

Ireland

Wales

Great Britain

London

! Ley lines link special places all over Britain.

Why Do That?

Some places are built to be holy or special. If we don't know why they have been built, they can seem very strange and mysterious. Why are there tunnels that lead nowhere inside one of the pyramids in Egypt? Who built a maze of caves and tunnels in a hill in North America 4,000 years ago? Very strange!

The Ghost of Versailles

In 1901, two English women from Oxford University visited the French palace of Versailles near Paris. During their visit, they got lost and saw scenes that they later found out had taken place in 1789. They saw the queen, Marie Antoinette, and they crossed a bridge that no longer existed in 1901. Had they somehow slipped through time on their trip?

! People claim they've seen the ghost of Marie Antoinette at the palace of Versailles.

Drowned Cities

Around the world, the remains of lost towns and cities lie hidden under the sea. Some lie far beneath the waves and are never seen except by divers. Others are uncovered at low tides.

Long Lost Civilizations

The first cities recorded by historians were built about 5,000 years ago in the Middle East. Yet some ruins that have been discovered are much older than this. Perhaps when the ice melted at the end of the last **ice age** 10,000 years ago, the rising seas swallowed up cities near the coast.

! There are hundreds of lost cities under the sea that have not been explored.

Stones Under the Sea

A huge object shaped like a horseshoe lies under the sea off the coast of Poompuhar, India. The seabed it stands on was dry land 11,000 years ago. Divers who have investigated think it is a man-made structure. If it is, it would be 6,000 years older than the first known city.

Looking for Atlantis

Nearly 2,500 years ago, the Greek writer Plato described a great lost city called Atlantis. He said it had been destroyed in a great column of fire, ash, and smoke hundreds or thousands of years earlier. The ruins of Atlantis disappeared beneath the sea. People have searched for traces of Atlantis ever since. Some think it might be a Greek island that was destroyed by a volcano that erupted 3,500 years ago.

! This is an artist's impression of what the city of Atlantis might have looked like.

Fields

Bridge

River

Homes

City of Spirits

Nearly 2,000 years ago, Nan Madol was a busy city on the island of Pohnpei in the Pacific Ocean. It was built on 92 artificial islands with canals for streets. Now, the deserted city is submerged beneath the waves.

Long Gone

The eerie underwater ruins are littered with 400,000 massive stone logs. No one knows how the ancient islanders moved and worked with such huge stones. Today people on Pohnpei live in huts with grass roofs. What could have happened to their **ancestors** and their great city?

SCIENCE SPOT

Scientists have found at least 200 mystery cities under the waters of the Mediterranean Sea. Using sonar, they bounce sound waves off the seabed and build sonar maps from the echoes, revealing long-dead places hidden for hundreds of years.

! Nan Madol has been called a "city of spirits"— a spooky silence now fills the empty houses.

Lost Treasures

One explorer, Johan Kubary, stole priceless **relics** from Nan Madol. The ship he used to move them sank, and the treasures have been lost to the sea. They will probably never be found again. Tales of their splendor only add to the mystery of Nan Madol.

! Nan Madol stretches over 10 square miles (26 sq km) of land and sea.

MYSTERY MOMENT

Japanese divers searched near Nan Madol for pearls in the early 1940s. Instead of finding pearls, they found platinum coffins in an underwater area known as the House of the Dead. Inside the coffins were skeletons measuring 6.5 feet (2 m) tall, far larger than the average height of the islanders. Were tall ancient islanders the secret to Nan Madol's giant architecture?

Mysteries of the Desert

Ancient Egyptians built the pyramids and sphinx over 4,550 years ago. The pyramids line up with the stars, and hide strange secrets that are still not understood.

Looking to the Skies

Pyramids are scattered around the Nile River. In 1983, Robert Bauval realized they match the positions of the stars of the **constellation** of Orion, the hunter. Two more pyramids are needed to complete the pattern—maybe they are still buried deep under the desert sand. The Nile River is in the same position as the Milky Way, the pale band of stars running across the night sky.

MYSTERY SITE

What: Pyramids

Where: Egypt

Why: They line up with the stars.

! It is said the positions of the pyramids match the pattern of the stars called Orion.

! The Great Pyramid at Giza is so well made that there's only a difference of 4 inches (10 cm) on each side. And each side is 755 feet (230 m) long!

Older than Expected

Using a computer to show how the stars looked long ago, Bauval worked out that the last time the stars lined up exactly like the pyramids was 12,500 years ago. This might be the time that ancient Egyptians called the "first time," when they believed men and gods walked together on the Earth. How did the Egyptians know the positions of the stars 12,500 years ago?

SCIENCE SPOT

There are other places around the world where parts of buildings seem to line up with the positions of stars as they were 12,500 years ago. One is Angkor Thom in Cambodia. The temple matches the positions of the stars in the constellation Draco, the Dragon.

Angkor Thom was built 900 years ago, but seems to follow patterns of the stars from 12,500 years ago.

Empty Pyramid

The pyramids were built to hold the dead bodies of the Egyptian pharaohs. Each pharaoh had his own pyramid, with gold and goods to help him in the **afterlife**. But the pyramid at Cheops has no pharaoh. There is only an empty coffin. No one knows what happened to the body.

Tunnels to Nowhere

There are more mysteries at Cheops. Four strange tunnels run inside the pyramid. Two of them have no openings to the outside. One tunnel is only 8 inches (20 cm) wide and is blocked by a slab of stone. No one knows what lies behind it, or the purpose of the four narrow tunnels.

MYSTERY MOMENT

Many people believe the dead pharaohs put a curse on their tombs so that bad things would happen to anyone who broke into them. In the years after the explorers Lord Carnarvon and Howard Carter opened the tomb of Tutankhamun in 1923, many of the people involved died of illness or in accidents. Were they victims of the mummy's curse?

Riddle of the Sphinx

The sphinx is a huge carved lion, with a face that looks human. It is in the Egyptian desert near the pyramids. It may be 7,000 years old. In 1995, scientists discovered that there may be tunnels and a chamber underground, 16 feet (5 m) beneath the paws of the sphinx. But this discovery was not as new as it seemed.

Ancient Secrets

In 1935, an American named Edgar Cayce claimed he had strange powers and had lived a previous life in ancient Egypt. He said there was a chamber beneath the sphinx. He said that he learned about it and the secrets kept there when he lived in Egypt thousands of years ago. He claimed that people from Atlantis had helped the Egyptians to build the sphinx and that evidence for this is in the secret chamber.

! The sphinx lay buried under the sand for thousands of years.

MYSTERY MOMENT

New South Wales, Australia, is over 9,000 miles (14,500 km) from Egypt. Yet a cave in New South Wales has a story carved into the rock in Egyptian **hieroglyphs**. The tale tells of Egyptian sailors whose boat was lost at sea and who ended up in the unknown land of Australia, unable to get home and with no idea where they were.

Spaced-Out Spaces

At least 4,000 years ago, people made huge objects from stone. It is hard to imagine how these were made using simple tools. Some suggest that extra-terrestrials—aliens from space—visited Earth long ago and helped.

Big Heads

Easter Island in the Pacific Ocean has over 800 giant stone heads looking out to sea. They were made more than 1,500 years ago and are 33 feet (10 m) tall. All the trees were cut down to use as rollers for moving the stones. With no trees, hunting and farming became difficult. Food ran out and the people started to kill and eat each other. They smashed some of the stone heads in revenge.

! No one knows why these stone heads line Easter Island and face out to sea.

Sky High

The desert in Nazca, Peru, is decorated with huge **geometric** designs and pictures of animals and birds. They have been made by picking up stones from the ground to show dust of a different color underneath—and they can only be seen from the air! The oldest were made 2,000 years ago, long before anyone on Earth had a plane or flying machine. Did the Nazca people make them for their gods to look down on from the sky or to help aliens to land?

! Some people think these shapes in the desert were made for visitors from space who used them to find Nazca as they came in to land.

MYSTERY SITE

What: Huge pictures in the ground

Where: Nazca, Peru

Why: The whole picture can only be seen from high in the sky.

Mystery Ruins

Huge chunks of stone cover the desert in Bolivia, South America. They are the remains of the city of Puma Punku, destroyed by an earthquake. The city once had a pyramid, temples, a **wharf**, and other buildings. The largest block of stone weighs as much as 600 cars, and comes from a **quarry** 10 miles (16 km) away.

! These huge blocks of stone would have been impossible to move when the city of Puma Punku was built thousands of years ago.

Modern Technology

Yet when the buildings were made 2,500 years ago, the local people had only small reed boats; they could not have moved the stones from the quarry to where the city is. The blocks are skillfully cut to fit together exactly. Even engineers today, with the latest modern equipment, would find it difficult to match them.

SCIENCE SPOT

✦ An iron pillar more than 23 feet (7 m) high in Delhi, India, has stood for more than 1,600 years, but there is not a spot of rust on it. The metal is very pure and would have been extremely difficult to make. It could not have been melted using just a coal fire—so how did Indian craftsmen make something so extraordinary? No one really knows.

! Kailasa was carved from solid rock more than 1,300 years ago.

Alien Help?

Kailasa Temple in India is carved from the solid rock of a hillside. It is decorated with carvings of elephants, human figures, and gods. Kailasa is now bare stone, but long ago it was covered with white plaster and brightly painted. This is such an amazing achievement that some people think aliens might have helped build it.

Fantastic Carving

Kailasa was started 1,300 years ago and took 150 years to build. More than 7,000 workers chipped away at the rock very slowly, using small chisels. They took away 220,000 tons (200,000 t) of stone. Local stories say the plan for the temple was given to the builders by aliens. The floor plan follows patterns of the stars in the sky over India.

Where Miracles Happen

In some places, strange events have happened that can't be explained by science. Religious people say these are miracles and that they are the work of gods or saints.

The Virgin Mary at Lourdes

In 1858, a girl named Bernadette Soubirous said a strange lady appeared to her in a **vision** at a **grotto**, or cave, near Lourdes in France. She saw the lady 18 times. No one else saw the vision. Because of the things Bernadette reported, the Catholic Church decided the lady was the Virgin Mary, the mother of Jesus. Now, there are several churches at Lourdes and five million **pilgrims** visit each year.

MYSTERY SITE

What: A spring
Where: Lourdes, France
Why: It is believed miracles can happen here.

Sick people visit Lourdes hoping for a **miracle**.

Water from Mud

One day, the lady told Bernadette to drink water from the spring at the grotto, but there was no spring. Bernadette dug in the dirt with her hands and tried to drink the muddy water she found. A few days later, a clear spring appeared where she had dug.

Miracle Cures

Bernadette is said to have been cured of **asthma** by drinking from the spring. Sick people came to the spring at Lourdes believing that drinking from it would cure them. So far, 67 people say they have been cured of various illnesses after drinking the spring water.

! The spring water at Lourdes now comes from a tap.

MYSTERY MOMENT

After her death, Bernadette's body was dug up three times. It had not **decayed** at all. Her body is now kept in a glass-topped coffin where pilgrims can see it. Although she died more than 140 years ago, her body is still intact. The church says this is a miracle.

The Lady of Fatima

Three children working as shepherds in the village of Fatima, Portugal, saw the Virgin Mary in visions, too. She appeared to them on the 13th day of the month for six months in 1917. One girl, Lucia Santos, said the lady shone "brighter than the sun, shedding rays of light clearer and stronger than a crystal glass filled with the most sparkling water . . ."

Spinning Sun

On the day of the last vision, the lady had promised a miracle for everyone to see, so that they would believe the children. More than 30,000 people turned up to watch. The sun seemed to spin with colored lights and move around in the sky for 10 minutes. Some people were terrified, thinking the world was going to end. Scientists had no explanation for what happened.

! Two million pilgrims visit the church at Fatima each year.

Miracle Gods

A statue of the Hindu god, Lord Ganesha, in a temple in New Delhi, India, apparently started to drink milk from a spoon in September 1995. Soon, statues of gods all over northern India seemed to be drinking milk. Some shops ran out of milk as people flocked to buy it to try the miracle themselves. Pilgrims rushed to see the milk-drinking statue. It stopped drinking later the same day.

! Hindus offer milk to a statue and hope to see a miracle.

MYSTERY MOMENT

When a tsunami flooded southeast Asia in 2004, all the buildings in many areas were destroyed by the water. In some places, though, the **mosques** were the only buildings left standing. Some **Muslims** believed **Allah** had protected the holy buildings in a miracle.

Mystery Hill

A strange network of caves and tunnels in Mystery Hill near Boston, Massachusetts was built about 4,000 years ago. Its purpose is unknown and we don't know who could have made it.

Stone in an Age of Wood

The Native American people living in the area around Boston 4,000 years ago only built with wood—never stone. But the buildings on Mystery Hill are made only of stone. Some of the structures are similar to temples in Greece and Malta, and some people think they may have been built by ancient Greeks who somehow got to North America. But there is no other evidence that people from the Mediterranean came to America so long ago.

MYSTERY SITE

What: Mystery Hill

Where: Boston, MA

Why: Built in a way that was unknown at the time

! Some of the stones and structures at Mystery Hill line up with the stars, so it may have been used as an **observatory.**

Stones and Sacrifice

There are caves that look like temples, and others with unknown uses. A stone slab with four legs was probably used to **sacrifice** victims. The table has channels at the edge that could be gutters to carry away the blood. Underground, beneath the sacrifice table, is a stone room where a priest may have hidden and spoken. It would seem like the voice of a god, speaking from deep under the ground.

! Underground passageways and rooms at Mystery Hill could have been used by a priest.

MYSTERY MOMENT

Stonehenge (above) in England is another place where religious rituals and sacrifices may have been carried out. It was built around the same time as Mystery Hill. Stonehenge is a circle of huge stones, with horizontal stones balanced on top. Some of the stones weigh up to 50 tons (45 t). The stones would have been incredibly difficult to cut and move with only simple tools 4,000 years ago.

The Money Pit

When Daniel McGinnis discovered the site of a strange pit in 1795, he thought he would dig up treasure. He had no idea that he had uncovered a mystery that would remain unsolved for more than 200 years.

Hidden Treasure

Out hunting, McGinnis found a clearing in the trees. It looked as if the ground had been cleared and a pit dug and refilled fairly recently. He wondered what might be buried there. He and his friends started to dig. It was not easy; they dug 26 feet (8 m) before they gave up.

Severed Hand

Rumors soon sprang up that the pit held pirate treasure. It became known as the Money Pit. Though many people have tried to reach the bottom of the pit since, no one has succeeded. A video camera lowered into the shaft showed grainy pictures of what may be wooden chests and a severed human hand.

! In 1971, diggers tried to find treasure in the money pit.

Not Just a Hole in the Ground

You would think it would be easy to get to the bottom of a deep hole with modern drilling equipment and robots. But the Money Pit was built very carefully. Every 10 feet (3 m), a barrier of wood, clay, or stone crosses the shaft. And the pit is connected by a tunnel to a nearby **cove** so that it floods at high tide. Even the beach at the cove is false, added just to cover the drainage tanks that flood the pit.

Deep Mystery

The pit is far too complicated for pirates to have dug. Some people think it might be much older than the pirate story suggests. There is an odd arrangement of stones in the shape of a cross not far from the Money Pit. Many think the pit might hide the Holy Grail, the cup used by Jesus at his last supper.

! There are barriers at different levels of the pit, and a tunnel that floods it at high tide.

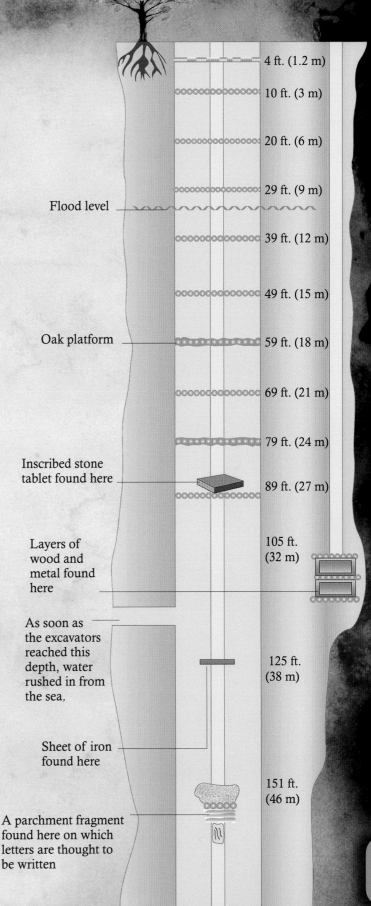

4 ft. (1.2 m)

10 ft. (3 m)

20 ft. (6 m)

29 ft. (9 m)

Flood level

39 ft. (12 m)

49 ft. (15 m)

Oak platform — 59 ft. (18 m)

69 ft. (21 m)

79 ft. (24 m)

Inscribed stone tablet found here — 89 ft. (27 m)

Layers of wood and metal found here — 105 ft. (32 m)

As soon as the excavators reached this depth, water rushed in from the sea.

125 ft. (38 m)

Sheet of iron found here

151 ft. (46 m)

A parchment fragment found here on which letters are thought to be written

25

Is Anybody There?

Not all lost places are beneath the sea. There are tales of places on land that once existed and have mysteriously vanished, or places from which all the people have disappeared without a trace.

Iron Gates in the Hillside

A old English tale tells of a farmer riding a white horse to sell at market at Alderley Edge, England, when an old man appeared and offered to buy the horse. The old man struck a rock, which split to reveal iron gates. The two men went through the gates.

! Does the beautiful countryside at Alderley Edge contain something strange?

MYSTERY SITE

What: Mysterious cave

Where: Alderley Edge, England

Why: Strange tales and buried treasure

Sleeping Knights

Here were caves with tunnels lined with knights in armor sleeping with their horses. One knight had no horse. The last cave was heaped with treasure. The old man told the farmer to take the price he wanted for his horse and leave.

Lying in Wait

The farmer believed he had seen the sleeping knights of King Arthur, ready to awake and defend England in a time of extreme danger. Although he searched, the farmer could never find the iron gates again. No one else has found the entrance since.

! A white horse, an old man, and hidden tombs are part of the Alderley Edge mystery.

MYSTERY MOMENT

Although no one has been able to find the iron gates again, people have found gold bars near Alderley Edge. The first was found in the 1960s, but kept secret. Then another four were found in the 1990s. The gold bars are very old and weigh about 3 1/2 pounds (1.5 kg) each. No one has been able to find out where they originally came from. Could they be from the hidden treasure cave?

The Lost Colony

English explorer Walter Raleigh helped set up the first British **colony** in North America at Roanoke in North Carolina. In 1587, 100 men, women, and children settled there, and the **governor** left for a trip to England. When he returned three years later, there was no trace of the colonists—they had all vanished. No one ever found them or their bodies. Later it was discovered that some native American groups living in the area had pale skin and blue eyes; perhaps they were descended from the lost colonists.

! Gatehouse entrance to the recreation of Fort Raleigh on Roanoke Island

SCIENCE SPOT

In 1542, the Spanish explorer Francisco de Orellana searched South America for a lost city of gold. He said he found villages and towering cities. When people returned 100 years later, they found only small tribes of hunters. Scientists say the soil in this area shows evidence that people really did live there. Could a great **civilization** crumble to nothing without a trace in 100 years?

Buried Empire

The first emperor of China had a huge burial mound made to hold his body when he died. Inside, he had a copy of his empire built with miniature palaces, a jeweled sky, and flowing rivers. The burial mound is said to be fitted with traps to kill anyone who tried to break in. The builders were killed so they could not tell anyone how to enter the mound. The mound has never been explored.

! The first Chinese emperor had a large terra-cotta army of life-size pottery soldiers buried nearby to guard his secret tomb.

MYSTERY MOMENT

The deserted ruins of villages around the San Pedro River in Colorado are the only sign that 700 years ago people lived here. The Anasazi people fled the area in the late 1200s—but no one knows why. The people carefully sealed the buildings and stores before they left.

Glossary

afterlife	a life after death that some people believe exists
Allah	the Arabic word for god, used to mean the Muslim god
ancestors	members of a family who died long ago
asthma	a medical condition that makes it difficult to breathe sometimes
civilization	society that has developed enough to have built towns and cities
colony	a group of people who leave their country to settle in a new area
constellation	a group of stars that forms a pattern or picture
cove	a small bay on the coast
decayed	rotted away
geometric	made up of simple shapes such as squares, triangles, and circles
governor	leader of a place or group of people
grotto	cave
hieroglyphs	the writing used in ancient Egypt in which pictures stood for words
ice age	a period when the Earth was colder than it is now, and ice covered areas which are now ordinary land and sea
ley lines	lines which may be drawn between certain places that some people believe carry strange forms of energy
miracle	a strange event that cannot be easily explained and which some people believe is caused by a god

mosques	places of worship for Muslims
Muslim	person who follows the religion of Islam
observatory	a place for looking at the stars and planets
pilgrims	people who visit a holy place to pray to or praise their god
quarry	a place for digging out stone
relics	valuable items from a long time ago
sacrifice	something offered to a god
sonar map	a map made by measuring sound echoes bounced off the ground or seabed
sound waves	energy that carries sound
vision	something seen that appears to be real but is really some kind of spiritual or mental experience
wharf	a landing place where boats and ships load and unload goods

Index

Web Finder

www.mysteriousplaces.com
Photos of ancient places surrounded by mystery, with explanations of what is strange about them

www.unmuseum.com/odd.htm
More information about lots of the places mentioned in the book, and some others

www.pbs.org/wgbh/nova/easter
Describes Easter Island and the archaeologists who work to uncover its mystery